SEASONAL SCIENCE PROJECTS

Summer

Science Projects

JOHN WILLIAMS

Evans

Spring Science Projects
Summer Science Projects
Autumn Science Projects
Winter Science Projects

Published by Evans Brothers Ltd
2A Portman Mansions
Chiltern Street
London W1M 1LE
England

First published in 1996

ISBN 0 237 51383 8

Acknowledgements
Planning and production by The Creative Publishing Company
Edited by Paul Humphrey
Designed by Christine Lawrie
Commissioned photography by Chris Fairclough
Illustrations by Jenny Mumford
The publishers would like to thank the staff and pupils of East Oxford First School for their help in the
preparation of this book.

For permission to reproduce copyright material, the author and publishers gratefully acknowledge
the following: Bruce Coleman Ltd: 6 (top), 8 (MPL Fogden), 14 (Massimo Borchi), 16 (Thomas Bucholz),
18 (Fritz Prenzel), 24 (Gerald Cubitt); Christine Osborne Pictures: 26; Oxford Scientific Films: 11 (Martyn
Colbeck); Alex Ramsay: 6 (bottom).

Contents

* Words in bold in the text are explained in the glossary.

What is summer?

There are four seasons — spring, summer, autumn and winter. Summer is the hottest season of the year.

Here are two signs that summer has come:
■ There are flowers blooming in parks and gardens.
■ It stays light until quite late in the evening.
Can you think of any more?

Right: For both players and spectators light, white clothes are best in summer.
Below: A garden in full summer bloom.

In the summer people often wear white or light coloured clothes. This project will help you understand why.

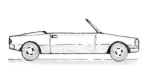

PROJECT: Colour and temperature

You will need
- Shallow lids from two boxes, for example, shoe boxes
- About 1kg of black powder paint
- About 1kg of plaster of Paris powder
- 2 soil thermometers

What to do

1. Fill one box lid with a 3cm thick layer of powder paint and the other with a 3cm layer of plaster of Paris powder.

2. Place the two box lids on the ground outside, or on a sunny windowsill.

3. Use the soil thermometers to measure the temperature of the powders every hour for one or two days.

Which box gets warmest?

Draw a chart like this one to show the differences in temperature.

Time	Temperature in °C	
	Black box	White box
9.00am		
10.00am		
11.00am		

Go out into the school car park on a hot day. Feel the cars. Which ones are warmer to the touch, the dark coloured ones or the light coloured ones?

Why do you think some colours get hotter than others?

Hot air rises

Hot air rises. Even small amounts of air warmed by a radiator will float upwards. Large amounts of moving warm air are called **thermals.**

These balloons float because they are filled with hot air.

Project: Make a hot air balloon

You will need
- Five sheets of tissue paper each about 75cm x 50cm
- A pencil
- Scissors
- Glue
- A hair dryer

What to do

1. Fold a sheet of paper in half. Then in half again and then in half again.

2. Unfold the sheet to show a pattern. Use the pattern to cut out the shape shown in the diagram opposite.

3. Repeat these steps for three of the other sheets. These are the sides of your balloon.

4. Cut a 50cm square from the fifth piece of tissue paper. This will be the top of your balloon.

5. Glue the four sides to the edges of this square.

6. Hold the sides of the balloon together and stick them with glue.

7. Cut a 25cm square of tissue paper. Cut a hole in the middle. Stick this square to the bottom of the balloon.

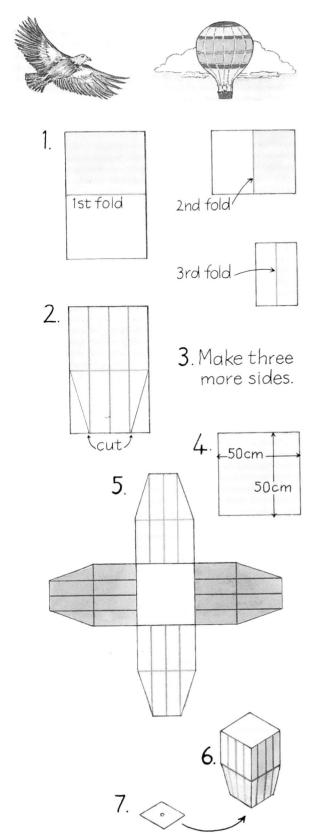

1.

1st fold

2nd fold

3rd fold

2.

3. Make three more sides.

cut

4. ←50cm→ 50cm

5.

6.

7.

8. Place the nozzle of the hair dryer in the hole at the base of the balloon and blow hot air into it. Hold it there for several minutes until you feel the tug of the balloon.

9. When the sides of the balloon are quite hot, let it go. How high does it fly?

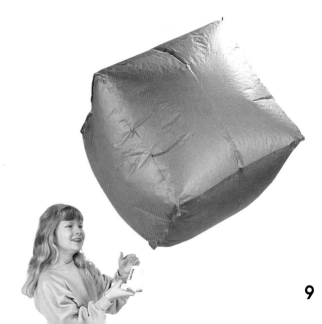

9

Evaporation

After it has rained, the trees, grass and playgound are very wet. When the sun shines everything dries out again. This experiment will help you find out how quickly the sun dries things.

PROJECT: Drying a puddle

You will need
- A playground puddle
- A piece of chalk
- A sunny day!

What to do

1. Draw around the edge of the puddle with the chalk. Mark the time next to the chalk outline.

2. Come back every hour, marking the new outline and time, until the puddle has disappeared.

How long did the puddle take to dry? Where do you think the water in the puddle has gone?

 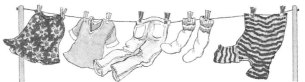 

When it is very hot our bodies sweat. As the sweat **evaporates**, it cools us down. Very large animals need more than sweat to keep themselves cool. Elephants have ears that act like car **radiators**. They spread out their ears so that the wind can cool the blood that runs through them.

The wind can also help to dry things as this project will show.

PROJECT: Drying in the wind

You will need
- Some pieces of cotton cloth, all 30cm x 30cm
- Clothes pegs

What to do

1. Soak all the pieces of cloth in water. Do not squeeze the water out.

2. Peg them on to fences or on trees in different parts of the playground or garden. Make sure you peg them: in the shade; in the sun; in the shade with the wind; in the sun with the wind. You could also hang some indoors.

Which one takes longest to dry? Which one dries the quickest?

The salty sea

Many people like to take holidays by the sea in summer. We know that there is salt in sea water because we can taste it when we swim. We can't see the salt because the little pieces in the water are too small.

PROJECT: Getting salt from sea water

You will need
- Salt
- A container of water
- Several plastic saucers
- A magnifying glass
- A clear plastic bag

What to do

1. Stir salt into the container of water until all of it has disappeared.

2. Pour the salt water carefully into each of the saucers and stand the saucers outside in the sun or on a sunny windowsill.

3. When the saucers are dry, look at what is left in them under a magnifying glass.

What you can see are **crystals** of salt. What shape are the crystals? Can you explain what has happened?

Do this experiment again using different amounts of salt. Try using other mixtures, like sugar or bath crystals. Do they work in the same way as salt?

Now repeat the experiment but this time place a clear plastic bag over the saucer. You can tuck the plastic bag under the saucer to stop it blowing away.

What do you notice appearing on the inside of the plastic bag as the water in the saucer dries up?

You are seeing the water cycle in action. The picture below shows you how it works in real life.

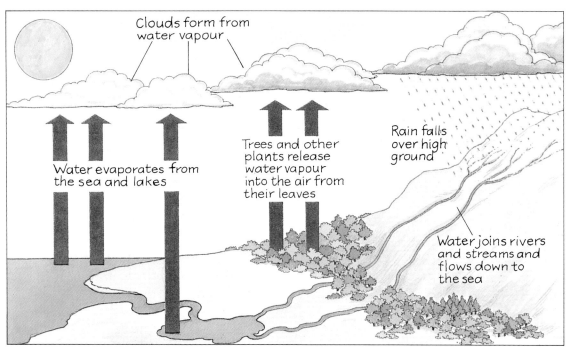

Clouds form from water vapour

Water evaporates from the sea and lakes

Trees and other plants release water vapour into the air from their leaves

Rain falls over high ground

Water joins rivers and streams and flows down to the sea

Floating in the sea

Swimming in the sea is easier than swimming in fresh water. Ships float at different levels in salt and fresh water, too. This experiment shows how salt in the water helps keep us and ships afloat.

It's easy to float in the Dead Sea because it is so salty.

PROJECT: Floating in the sea

You will need
- A drinking straw
- Plasticine
- 2 plastic aquarium tanks, one of fresh and one of salt water

What to do

1. Fix a small ball of Plasticine to the end of one of the drinking straws.

2. Put the straw in the tank of fresh water so that it floats upright.

3. Put a mark on the straw at the water level.

4. Now do the same for the tank of salt water.

How far apart are the marks on the straw? How much of the straw is under in fresh and in salt water?

Fill an aquarium with even saltier water and repeat the experiment. Does the extra salt make any difference?

Sailing boats

This is a sailing regatta in the Baltic Sea. How do the yachts manage to stay upright?

Summer is a good time for sailing model boats and real yachts. Racing yachts have long, thin **hulls** and tall sails.

How do they stay upright in the water when the wind is blowing and the sea is rough?

PROJECT: Testing hulls

You will need
- Two sheets of balsa wood, one 20cm long, 0.5cm thick and 10cm wide, and one 20cm long, 0.5 cm thick and 5cm wide
- Three pieces of wooden dowel, two 20cm long and one 35cm long
- Plasticine and sticky tape
- A modelling knife and metal ruler
- Some sheets of paper
- Scissors and a pencil

What to do

1. Cut a point at one end of each piece of balsa wood. These are your **bows**.

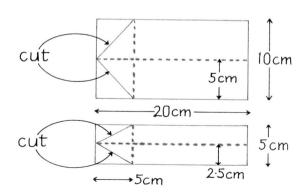

2. Use the pencil to make a hole in the middle of both pieces of wood 8cm from the bow. Push a 20cm dowel through each hole for masts.

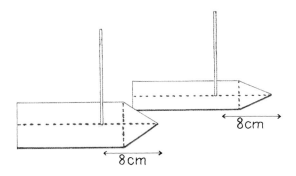

8cm

8cm

3. Make a paper sail for each boat and float them in water. Which one stays upright?

4. Replace the mast on the narrow boat with the longer dowel, leaving about 15cm under the boat.

5. Fix a small ball of Plasticine to the bottom of the dowel. Does the boat stay upright now?

Look at pictures of real yachts. What shape are the parts that are under the water?

WARNING: ASK AN ADULT TO HELP YOU CUT THE BALSA WOOD.

Catamarans

Catamarans have two hulls and trimarans have three.

Some sailing boats have more than one hull. Those that have two hulls are called catamarans. Those that have three are called trimarans.

PROJECT: Make a catamaran

You will need
- Two square-shaped plastic bottles
- A sheet of balsa wood 10cm wide, 0.5cm thick and 35cm long
- Four 35cm lengths of 1cm x 1cm balsa wood
- One piece of dowel about 40cm long
- Rubber bands
- A sheet of paper
- Scissors and sticky tape
- A pencil

What to do

1. Using the rubber bands, fix the sheet of balsa wood across the bottles. The bottles should be about 15 cm apart.

2. Fix the long square pieces of wood across each end of the bottles, on both the top and bottom, with more rubber bands.

3. Use the pencil to make a hole in the middle of the balsa wood. Fix the dowel mast into the hole.

4. Cut a sail from the sheet of paper. Stick it to the mast.

WARNING: ASK AN ADULT TO HELP YOU CUT THE BALSA WOOD.

Does your model float upright in the water?

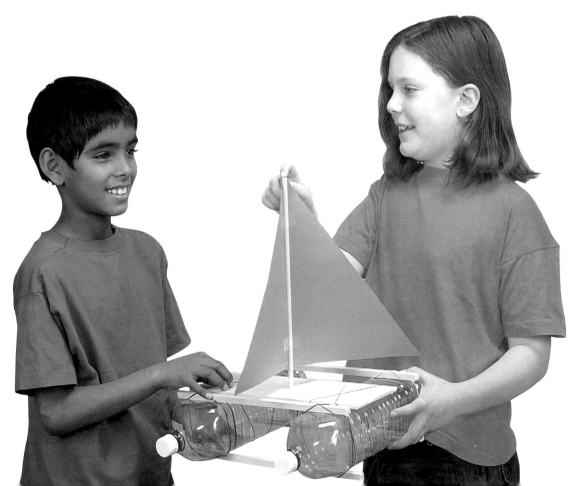

Plants in summer

All plants need water to stay alive. Sometimes, during a dry summer, we have to water our gardens with a watering can or hosepipe. Plants collect the water in the ground through their roots. Then it travels up through their stems.

Project: Plants in water

You will need
- Some white summer flowers like carnations or large daisies
- A jar full of water coloured with ink or food colouring

What to do

Place the flowers in the jar of coloured water and leave them there for a day. What happens to the colour of the flowers?

Try the experiment with different food colourings. Which ones work best?

Plants do not keep all the water they take in. Some of the water escapes through little holes in their leaves, called stomata. Stomata can close up during the day to help save water.

Project: Collecting water from plants

You will need
- A plant in a pot
- A plastic bag
- Sticky tape
- A watch

What to do

1. Put the plastic bag over the pot plant.

2. Fix the bag tightly around the stem of the plant with the sticky tape. Be careful not to damage the plant.

3. Measure the time it takes for water to collect on the inside of the bag.

4. Now fix a bag over just one leaf of another plant of the same type.

How much water comes from one leaf?

Try the experiment with a different plant. Does water appear in the bag at the same time?

Imagine how much water comes from a large tree or a forest of trees. Where does all the water go (see page 13)?

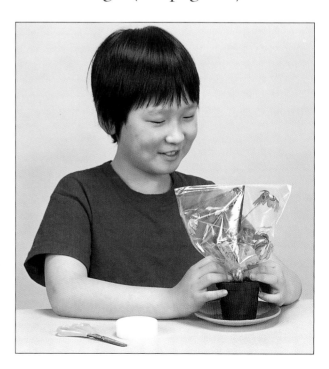

Plants need water

Summers can be very dry. Many plants have special leaves to help them keep the water inside. You can find out which leaves keep water the longest.

Project: Drying leaves

You will need
- Lots of different leaves
- Cotton thread
- Two short garden canes

What to do

1. Tie the thread between the canes. Then push the canes into the ground in a warm place where there is a breeze.

2. Tie the leaves on to the thread.

3. Look at the leaves every hour. Keep a record like this of how they change.

Changes in the leaf after every hour.	Type and shape of leaf	
	Holly	Oak
1 hour colour shape feel		
2 hours colour shape feel		

We have seen how plants both take in and let out water. You can make a small self-contained world where you can watch them doing this.

Project: Make a bottle garden

You will need

- A large plastic sweet jar with a wide neck
- A pack of clean potting soil from a garden centre
- Charcoal and small pebbles
- Some small plants like ivy, ferns and mosses
- About 250ml of water

What to do

1. Spread the pebbles on the bottom of the jar. Then put a layer of charcoal on top of the pebbles.

2. Sprinkle about 10cm of soil on to the charcoal.

3. Carefully take your plants out of their pots and plant them in the soil.

4. Water the soil but don't make it too wet.

5. Replace the lid and put your bottle garden in a warm, bright place, but not in direct sunlight.

Your plants should need no further attention.

23

Watering the fields

All crops need water or they will die. In countries where the summers are very dry water has to be brought up from wells deep underground.

The water can be pumped up by hand, by animal power, by a windmill or by a machine.

You can make a cardboard model of a hand pump.

At this traditional 'Persian well' in India, the oxen provide the power to lift the water.

PROJECT: A model hand pump

You will need
- Thin card
- Paper fasteners
- Crayons or felt-tip pens
- Scissors
- A pencil
- A ruler

What to do

1. Cut a piece of card for the backing 20cm x 18cm.

2. Cut a handle 20cm long and 3cm wide. Cut a piston 14cm long, 2cm wide along most of its length and 3cm wide at the end. Colour them both.

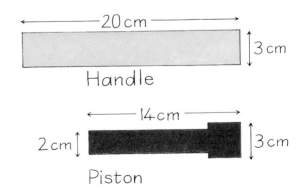

Handle

Piston

3. Make a hole in the handle, 1cm from the end and another 6cm from the end.

4. Make a hole in the backing card about 4cm in from the left hand side and 3cm from the top.

5. Fix the handle on to the backing card with a paper fastener.

6. Make a hole in the top of the piston. Then lay it in position over the handle. Mark and cut out two slits about two-thirds of the way down the backing card.

7. Thread the piston up through the slits. Fix it to the handle with a paper fastener.

8. Draw the well shaft on the backing paper. Colour the water blue.

What happens to the piston when you move the handle up and down?

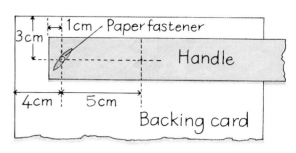

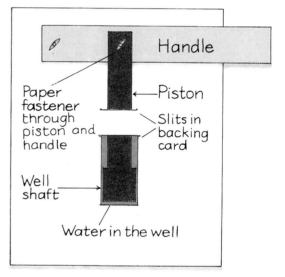

What would happen to the water in a real well if a piston was pushed down?

A shadoof

In some countries, like Egypt and India, a simple lever is used to bring water up from wells underground. The water is then used to **irrigate** the fields. The lever is called a shadoof and has been in use for thousands of years.

You can make your own model shadoof.

This Egyptian man is using a shadoof to raise water from a well to water his crops. The weight of water is balanced by the rocks at the other end of the lever.

PROJECT: Make a shadoof

You will need

- 3 pieces of 1cm x 1cm balsa wood, two 8cm long and one 18cm long
- A piece of thick card or balsa wood 10cm x 10cm
- Plasticine
- Scissors
- About 20cm of cotton thread
- A long pin or needle
- Glue
- A small piece of kitchen foil

What to do

1. Push the pin through the top of one of the short pieces of wood 2cm from the end.

2. Now push the pin through the long piece of wood about 5cm from the end. This piece will form the lever.

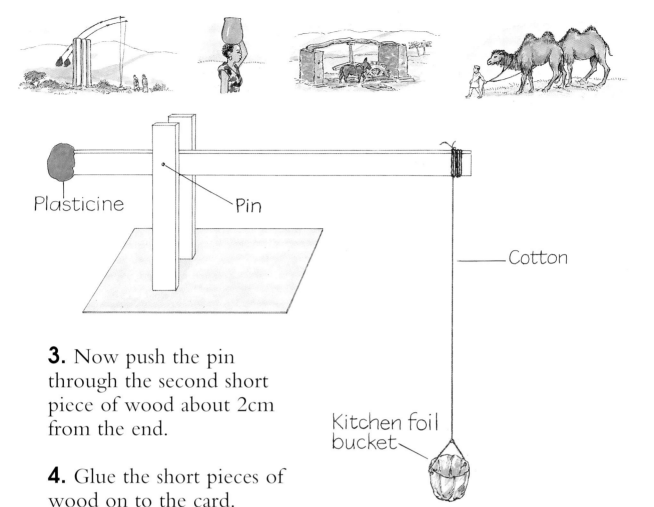

Plasticine

Pin

Cotton

3. Now push the pin through the second short piece of wood about 2cm from the end.

4. Glue the short pieces of wood on to the card.

Kitchen foil bucket

5. Glue or tie the cotton to the long end of the lever.

6. Make a little bucket from the piece of kitchen foil and tie or glue this to the other end of the cotton thread.

7. Balance the lever at its short end with Plasticine.

When the lever is balanced a heavy bucket of water can be lifted easily.

Notes for teachers and parents

Colour and temperature (Pages 6-7)

Objects receive heat from the sun through the process of radiation. It is the infrared radiation from the sun that warms us. This kind of radiation behaves in the same way as light, and can even be reflected and focused by a mirror. Shiny surfaces are good reflectors, while dull surfaces absorb the heat. Conversely, dull surfaces are better emitters of heat than shiny surfaces. Hence a hot liquid will retain its heat better in a shiny container than in a dark one. This should be understood when measuring the temperature of the two 'soils'. The temperature just above the surface may be similar — the light coloured one because of the reflection of heat, and the dark coloured one because of the heat emitted from it. However, the temperature inside the 'soils' should show a difference.

Hot air rises (Pages 8-9)

Children may understand that hot air rises, but they may not know why. As with other substances, heated air molecules vibrate more vigorously, and draw apart from one another. In this way, warm air becomes lighter and will rise up and float above cold, denser air. The hot air in the balloon will actually have less molecules compared with the equivalent volume of air outside. So it will float upwards in just the same way as a boat floats on water.

Making a hot air balloon can give rise to many cross-curricular activities. Children can be given the opportunity to study technology and design, the history of flight, weather and even mathematics. When making the balloon, children can begin to understand the concept of volume. They can make connections between volume and surface area, and make calculations such as what happens to the volume if the dimensions of the balloon are doubled or halved.

Evaporation (Pages 10-11)

Evaporation is the changing of a liquid into a vapour. There is almost instant evaporation when a liquid boils, but of course it does not have to reach this temperature before evaporation takes place. When a substance is heated the molecules inside it vibrate more and more quickly. Some molecules near the surface of the liquid may have enough energy to escape. This can happen at any temperature, although obviously the hotter it is the quicker the rate of evaporation.

Children should understand that just because the water in the puddle reduces, it has not, as it may seem to them, disappeared into thin air. It has just changed its state. This is because it is the hotter molecules that escape, leaving behind the cooler ones. On a hot day this can keep us cool, but in cold, windy conditions it can be dangerous, and the heat loss can be very considerable. The action of the wind is always an important factor in the process of evaporation. Elsewhere in this book (**Plants need water**), there are examples of how plants protect their leaves from the wind. They try to create little pockets of humid air near the stomata. In the case of most animals, their problem is to stop themselves overheating in hot weather. The ears of an elephant act like a car radiator. As the ears spread out, the blood in the capillaries cools. Unlike the leaves of plants, any movement or air in these circumstances is welcome.

Salt from sea water (Pages 12-13)

This is another evaporation experiment. However the emphasis changes to discovering what solids remain when all the water is gone. It would be helpful if the children had some previous experience of dissolving solids in water. They will then already know that some solids will normally fully dissolve in water, so that none of the particles can be seen, and the original solid cannot easily be retrieved. Other substances, however, do not dissolve fully. Instead, they remain as small particles suspended in the water. These particles can easily be retrieved by filtration. Salt is a chemical that does dissolve in water. Filtration will have no effect on the solution. Once the water has evaporated away, however, the salt will remain, ideally as small, cube-shaped crystals.

The final experiment in this section should help reinforce the idea that the water is still around, although as a vapour and not a liquid. Like the water from the transpiration experiments later in the book, it is not until it cools down that it will condense back into water.

Floating in water (Pages 14-15)

Children may often experiment with a variety of objects to find out if they will float or sink, but it is unlikely that they will do more than list two sets. It is much more difficult to understand how things float, and it is unreasonable to expect young children to manage this concept. When an object is placed on water, gravity would normally pull it down. However, there is an opposing push or upthrust which may keep the object afloat. Children can feel this upthrust by trying to push a piece of wood or plastic underwater. This is not, however, the whole story. A brick weighing 2.5 kg placed in a tank of water will seem to lose at least a kilogram of its weight, but it will still sink. Only if the brick could be spread thinly over the water, so that the upthrust was greater per given area of brick, would it float.

Children do not have to understand the theory, but they can experiment with this idea. A lump of Plasticine dropped into a tank of water will sink. However, if it is formed into a saucer-shaped boat, it will float. Because salt water is more dense that fresh water, the upthrust will be greater. The drinking straws are a form of crude hydrometer. They will float higher in salt water and even higher in very salty water.

Stability in water (Pages 16–19)

These two sections are about stability in water, particularly sailing yachts, which often have a very slim hull, and yet have a tall mast and a large area of sail. Most sailing boats manage with ballast to stop them capsizing. Racing yachts, however, require a deep keel, often tipped with lead. When the wind pushes on one side of the sails, there is a push from the water on the opposite side of the keel, so keeping the boat upright. The experiments in this project will help children understand the technology. Catamarans are often more stable than craft with a single hull. Even with a basic model such as this, stability should not be a problem. Children can choose between two basic sail patterns — the square rig and the fore-and-aft rig. They should understand that all the various pushes and pulls of the wind on the sails, and the water on the boat, are all examples of forces.

NOTE: A modelling knife should always be used in conjunction with a metal ruler. Both as a safeguard and a guide, the blade should be held against the edge of the ruler.

Plants in summer (Pages 20–23)

These two sections look at how plants take in and lose water and how they avoid losing water during times of drought. Plants can lose as much as 90 per cent of their total water through transpiration. This is the loss of water, mainly through the stomata, that is necessary in order that other water can be drawn up the stem. The stomata have to stay open for at least part of the day, to allow the passage of oxygen and carbon dioxide during respiration and photosynthesis.

In times of water shortage, plants need to cut down on loss through transpiration. The xerophytes (eg cacti), are a very specialized group of plants, adapted to survive under extreme conditions. They have special water storage cells, their leaves are reduced to sharp spines and their stomata rarely open during the day. Other plants may not be so specialized, but they nonetheless often need to cope with temporary water shortages. One of the most common adaptations is a leathery and often waxy cuticle. The stomata is often at the base of a small pit, so protecting it from moving air. The holly is one such plant. Other ways in which plants cut down water loss is by having hair-like structures in the leaves, or to have folded or rolled up leaves. The oleander is a good example of a plant with a hairy leaf, while many grasses have rolled up leaves.

The terrarium should be a balanced plant community. It can include some small invertebrates, so as to make it into a biotope — a small area in which plants and animals with similar habitats can live together as a balanced ecological community.

Raising water (Pages 24–27)

In the first of these two sections a model shows how a piston works in conjunction with a lever handle. In a real pump there are two valves — one is the piston and one in the base of the barrel. When the piston moves down the lower valve closes, but the piston valve opens. When this happens, water enters the top of the pump and out of the spout. Because water is raised by atmospheric pressure, a pump of this kind cannot raise water by more than 10 metres. If children are aware of the three different kinds of levers they should be able to decide which type of lever is used for the handle of this model and whether other types of lever could be used instead.

Shadoofs can be found in use today along the banks of rivers in the Middle East, India and Egypt. They are used for raising water over a short distance and are based on the balanced lever principle. The shadoof is a type one lever, where the fulcrum is anywhere between the effort and the load. It is balanced so that it needs only a light touch to raise the load of water. Levers in general do not have to be balanced in this way, it just depends on what they are designed to do.

Notes on the National Curriculum

The specific references in this section are made to programmes of study. However, all the work in this book is compatible with the attainment targets for science, levels 1–5. Teachers will therefore be able to make their own judgements concerning individual pupils based on their ability to carry out these projects.

Experimental and investigative science
All the practical work in this book, the experimenting, testing and recording meet many of the requirements of this programme of study, at both key stages 1 and 2.

The details of other programmes of study are listed under individual sections.

What is summer?
Life processes and living things (key stages 1 and 2)
Materials and their properties (key stage 2)
Physical processes (key stage 2)
There are cross-curricular links with geography.

Hot air rises
Materials and their properties (key stages 1 and 2)
Physical processes (key stage 2)
There are cross-curricular links with technology and mathematics.

Evaporation *and* **The salty sea**
Materials and their properties (key stages 1 and 2)
Physical processes (key stages 1 and 2)
There are cross-curricular links with geography.

Floating in the sea *and* **Sailing boats**
Materials and their properties (key stages 1 and 2)
Physical processes (key stages 1 and 2)
There are strong cross-curricular links with technology.

Plants in summer *and* **Plants need water**
Life processes and living things (key stages 1 and 2)
Materials and their properties (key stage 2)
There are cross-curricular links with geography.

Watering the fields *and* **The shadoof**
Life processes and living things (key stages 1 and 2)
Physical processes (key stages 1 and 2)
There are cross-curricular links with technology, history, geography and R.E.

Further reading

Fitzgerald, Janet, *Science Through the Seasons: Summer in the Wood* (Evans, 1992)

Harlow, Rosie and Morgan, Gareth, *Fun With Science: The Seasons* (Kingfisher, 1991)

Pluckrose, Henry, *Changing Seasons* (Franklin Watts, 1993)

Woolfitt, Gabrielle, *Science Through the Seasons: Summer* (Wayland, 1995)

Association for Science Education, *Be Safe*, 2nd edition (1990)